WATERWORLDS

BY
BARBARA TAYLOR

A WORLD OF WATER

The still, smooth water of lakes and ponds; the sparkling white water of rushing rivers and bubbling streams; the muddy, smelly water of swamps, marshes and bogs – all these waterworlds are rich treasure-chests of hidden wildlife. They are fragile, ever-changing places, that provide plenty of food and shelter, especially for the young of animals such as insects and fish. Millions of birds nest and feed in these habitats alongside spectacular predators, such as alligators and tigers. Water is a perfect life-support system for the cells of living creatures, which are made of over 75 per cent water. Water contains oxygen for breathing and carbon dioxide for water plants to make their food. It also protects its inhabitants from wide swings in temperature because it heats up and cools down more slowly than the surrounding air.

FOOD ECHOES

Freshwater species of dolphin, such as these Amazon river dolphins, are almost blind because they don't need their eyes to find food in the cloudy, muddy river waters. Instead, they use echolocation – sending out high-pitched sounds and waiting for the echoes to bounce back from fish. The echoes tell them the shape of objects and how near they are.

TOO MUCH WATER

Aquatic plants and animals must have ways of stopping too much water getting inside their bodies. Water lilies, such as these massive Amazon lilies, have an extra tough, waxy coating on the upper surface of their leaves so the water runs off them. Their leaves are supported by the water and float on the surface, making good sunbathing platforms.

HIDDEN DANGER

The strong jaws of the alligator snapping turtle could easily bite off your finger. Luckily, it prefers to eat fish, luring them into its mouth with a built-in wriggly worm on its tongue. There are 200 or so species of freshwater turtles lurking at the bottom of lakes, rivers and swamps. They can stay submerged for long periods and some hibernate underwater for weeks at a time.

SNORKELS, AQUALUNGS AND GILLS

One of the most important factors in the life of aquatic animals is their oxygen supply. Hanging upside-down from the surface of the water, mosquito larvae take in oxygen from the air through a 'snorkel' at the rear end of the body. Other methods of obtaining oxygen include the 'aqualungs' or bubbles of air carried underwater by diving beetles, and the gills of fish, tadpoles and damselfly larvae, which allow oxygen from the water to diffuse directly into the animal's body.

WETLAND PEOPLES

Many people live near rivers, lakes and swamps so they can use them for water, food and transport. In this floating market in Thailand, people sell their fruit, vegetables and other produce from boats because the houses have canals of water flowing past them instead of roads. Waterways all over the world provide vital links for trade and transport.

SUPER DIVER

In fast-flowing water and strong currents, many animals and plants have adaptations that stop them being swept away. The torrent duck is completely at home diving into the foaming, rushing waters of rivers in the Andes to look for insect larvae to eat. It uses sharp spurs under its wings to cling to slippery rocks, while balancing and steering with its stiff tail. Its large webbed feet make it a powerful swimmer.

WETLANDS OF THE WORLD

LAKE BAIKAL

The deepest and oldest lake in the world is Lake Baikal in Siberia. It is at least 25 million years old and bigger than Belgium. It contains the world's largest volume of surface freshwater – more than that of North America's five Great Lakes put together. Lake Baikal contains a huge variety of unique wildlife. More than 1,000 of the species that live there are found nowhere else in the world.

Wetlands cover about six per cent of the Earth's surface, ranging from tiny mountain streams to vast flooded forests called swamps. They are found all over the world, wherever there is heavy rainfall or where water stays on the surface because it cannot drain away through frozen soil or impermeable rocks. Wetlands occur in every type of climate, including the frozen Arctic tundra; the hot, humid tropical rainforest; and the temperate regions in-between. The Okavango wetland wilderness even survives among the sands of the Kalahari Desert. Wetlands are often found along coasts, such as the mangrove swamps of tropical coasts or the saltmarshes of river estuaries. Huge areas of wetland occur on the lands drained by giant rivers. Wetlands are always changing as lakes and ponds dry up or fill in with plants, and saltmarshes or mangrove swamps gradually extend out to sea.

NORTH AMERICA

KEY

Wetland areas of the world

Areas mentioned in this book

1 Lake Baikal, Russia
2 The Camargue, France
3 The Okavango Delta, Botswana
4 The Amazon, Brazil
5 Malaysian Mangroves
6 Boglands of Europe
7 Sunderbans, Bangladesh
8 The Everglades, USA
9 Lake Victoria, E. Africa
10 Lake Tanganyika, E. Africa
11 Lake Nakuru, E. Africa
12 Norfolk Broads, Britain
13 Kakadu N.P. Australia
14 Coto Doñana, Spain

THE CAMARGUE

The famous white Camargue horses live on the salty marshes and shallow lakes of the River Rhône estuary in France. They eat a lot of marshland reeds and so halt the reeds' spread across areas of free water. This is essential for tens of thousands of swans, ducks and geese, as these waters provide food, winter homes and resting places during their migration.

MALAYSIAN MANGROVES

Mangrove swamps fringe the coasts of Malaysia and other tropical countries, holding together the sticky, squelchy mud with their dense arching roots. There is little oxygen in the mud, so the mangroves draw it in directly from the air through their roots. A whole army of creatures lives in and on the rich mud of mangrove swamps.

EUROPE

ASIA ①

⑥

⑫

②

⑭

AFRICA

⑦

⑤

⑨⑪
⑩

PACIFIC
OCEAN

ATLANTIC
OCEAN

③

INDIAN
OCEAN

AUSTRALIA

⑬

THE AMAZON RIVER

The second longest river in the world, the River Amazon, holds more than one fifth of the Earth's freshwater. About 2,000 species of fish live in the Amazon, as well as many reptiles, such as caimans and anacondas, and mammals such as the Amazonian manatee. When the Amazon floods, its waters create a unique area of flooded forest the size of England. In the Amazonian lowlands, this swamp forest, called igapo, is flooded for four to seven months of the year up to a height of 12 metres (40 ft).

THE OKAVANGO DELTA

Stretching over 20,000 sq km (7,700 sq miles) of the Kalahari Desert, in Botswana, the Okavango Delta provides a spectacular oasis for wildlife. It is home to hippos, crocodiles, lechwe, sitatunga and thousands of water birds, such as ducks, geese, herons, ibises and fish eagles. In the dry season, desert antelope mingle with wetland species such as waterbuck.

WETLAND PLANTS

F rom algae, mosses and water lilies to reeds, grasses and trees – hundreds of flowering and non-flowering plants grow well in wetlands. The water supports the weight of the plant, so there is no need for water plants to have strong stems. Water and nutrients float all around them in the water, so the roots of water plants tend to be small and either float freely or anchor the plant in the mud. They also do not have to survive such extreme temperatures as land plants. There are some disadvantages though. Oxygen and light may be hard to come by and flowering and seed production can be difficult, especially in times of flood or drought.

AIR PLANTS

The silvery bubbles along the leaves of this Canadian pondweed are bubbles of oxygen. It is given off as a by-product when the plant makes its food in a process called photosynthesis. There are more bubbles on sunny days because the plant needs the Sun's energy to make its food from water and carbon dioxide. Carbon dioxide in the water is taken in directly through the leaves of the plants. Canadian pondweed provides oxygen for plants and animals to breathe but it spreads quickly and can choke other plants.

WATER POLLINATION

A few plants, such as ribbon weed, rely on water for pollination.
This is a more risky process than pollination by insects.

1. Ripe male flowers float up to the surface of the water. They have a bubble of air inside them to help them float.

2. Male flowers are pushed along by the wind and water currents, and slide down into the female flower.

3. Once the female flower has been pollinated, it is pulled back under the water by the flower stalk.

4. Under the water, the pollinated flower ripens into a fruit, protected by the leaves.

GREEN CARPET

Tiny floating plants, such as duckweed, often carpet the surface of the water like grass on a lawn. Here, they do not compete for light with submerged water weeds or algae. Duckweeds are among the smallest and simplest flowering plants in the world. Tiny roots hang down from the leaves and absorb minerals from the water, and so they can grow in water that is too deep for plants to be rooted on the bottom.

MEAT-EATING PLANTS

To help them survive in the poor soil of bogs and marshes, carnivorous plants trap insects and other small animals to get extra nutrients. The yellow trumpet pitcher from the USA attracts insects with a glistening yellow-green hood covered with nectar glands. Insects fall down into the pitcher and are dissolved by digestive juices to make a soupy meal. The plant then absorbs its meal, which is full of nutrients, through the walls of the pitcher.

FLOWER FLAG

Yellow flag, like most water plants, produces its flowers above the surface of the water. It is pollinated by bumble bees, which crawl right inside the flower, following the lines called honey guides on the petals. These point the way to the nectar. As the bee crawls into the flower, it deposits the pollen it is carrying from other yellow flags onto the stigma, or female part of the flower. As the bee climbs out of the flower, it collects a new load of pollen from the anthers, or male part of the flower. The stigma curls out of the way to avoid receiving its own pollen.

LEAF SHAPES

Some water plants, such as water crowfoot, have two types of leaves – large, flat leaves that float on the surface and finely divided leaves under the surface. The fine submerged leaves offer less resistance to the current of fast-flowing rivers and streams. The leaves that float on the surface are good at catching the sunlight the plants need.

PEAT BOGS

Large areas in cooler parts of the world are covered in soggy, flat peat bogs (or mires) and fenlands. Bogs occur in Canada, Russia and most of Europe, especially Finland. Peat is formed when dead plant material only partly decomposes in waterlogged soil. This can happen around the edge of a lake or on higher ground where the rainfall is heavy and the rocks are hard and acidic. A bog can take up to 5,000 years to form. Few plants can tolerate the acidic conditions, although carnivorous plants, cotton sedges and cranberries are common. Waterlogged bogs are ideal places for aquatic insects and biting flies, which provide food for birds and frogs. Many birds nest on peat bogs, including snipe, redshank, curlews, plovers and divers. Hunting birds range from spectacular merlins and hobbies to short-eared owls and even golden eagles.

VACUUM CLEANERS

Bladderworts have small bladders or sacs on their thin, feathery underwater leaves. If aquatic insects brush against trigger hairs on the bladders, a trap door snaps open. Water is sucked into the bladder, carrying the insect with it. The bladderwort's trap works rather like a botanical vacuum cleaner.

MIRACLE MOSS

The most characteristic peat bog plant is sphagnum moss. This amazing bright green, bushy moss soaks up water like a huge bath sponge. It can absorb up to ten times its own weight in water. In the past, it was used to dress soldier's wounds and American Indians used dried sphagnum moss as nappies for babies. Today, it is used by gardeners to line hanging baskets and stop water from draining away too quickly. Sphagnum moss sucks nutrients out of the water and on peat bogs it makes the water even more acidic and poor in nutrients.

BOG BIRDS

Many waders, such as this curlew, nest in bogs because there are plenty of safe nesting sites and insects to eat. The mother and young are both well camouflaged to blend in with the vegetation and the fluffy chicks can run about as soon as they hatch. Birds also use peat bogs as winter resting places or feeding areas during migration journeys.

STICKY FLYPAPER

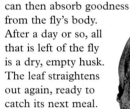

A fly provides a tasty snack and a welcome source of extra nutrients for this sundew plant. Special hairs on the leaves have sticky droplets on the ends. Insects are attracted to the glistening droplets and stick to the leaves like flies on flypaper. As the fly struggles, the leaf folds round it and hairs pour digestive juices over its body. The plant can then absorb goodness from the fly's body. After a day or so, all that is left of the fly is a dry, empty husk. The leaf straightens out again, ready to catch its next meal.

HOW A PEAT BOG FORMS

A peat bog may form when a lake fills in with mud and plants.

The water is clear, with mud on the bottom of the lake.

Silt and mud collect around plant roots. This build-up allows plants to grow across the lake.

Mosses grow, die and start to rot, building up layers of peat.

Bog mosses build up domes of peat above the level of the water. This is called a raised bog.

BOG BODIES

Over 1,000 ancient bodies have been found preserved in peat bogs in northern Germany, Scandinavia and Britain. The acid conditions and low levels of oxygen in the bogs prevented the bodies from decomposing. Oxygen is needed for decomposition to occur because the bacteria that break down plant and animal material need oxygen to survive. The acid peat is such a good preservative that it is possible to identify the last meal of a 2,000-year-old body, unearthed from the peat.

RIVER ANIMALS

As a river flows from the mountains to the sea, its moving water provides a variety of places for animals to feed and shelter. Insect larvae, worms, water snails and shrimps living on the river bed are snapped up by hungry fish, crayfish and turtles. The fish are, in their turn, hunted by otters, crocodiles and birds such as herons, dippers and kingfishers. Swallows and bats swoop low over the water to scoop up insects hatching from the water's surface. The moving water of rivers holds much more oxygen for animals to breathe than the still water of ponds and lakes. But river animals must avoid being washed away by the current or smashed against the rocks. They hide away in crevices, glue themselves to rocks or cling on tightly with hooks and suckers. In some rivers, muddy water may make it difficult for animals to navigate or catch food. Some animals, such as salmon and eels, spend only part of their life cycle in rivers, moving to the sea to breed or feed.

FLYING UNDERWATER

The dipper has the remarkable ability to walk underwater up the beds of fast-flowing streams to search for water insects, tadpoles and worms. Its tail acts as a hydroplane in the current to keep its feet firmly on the bottom. It also dives into the water from the air. The dipper is a good indicator that the water is clean. If pollution kills the insects that it feeds on, the dipper cannot survive.

SPECTACULAR SALMON

Salmon make long migration journeys from their feeding grounds in the sea to their breeding grounds in rivers. They usually return to the river where they themselves hatched, by recognizing the distinctive smell of the water. As they journey upriver, the salmon may have to leap up waterfalls. They make their best jumps from deep water because they can build up speed beforehand. Many jumps fail though and the salmon drop back exhausted.

STREAMLINED HUNTER

The shy and inquisitive otter is a land animal that spends much of its time in the water, particularly when feeding. Its fur is waterproof. An otter hunts for eels, trout and crayfish from dusk to dawn, detecting its prey by sight or using its whiskers to sense the vibrations made by fish as they swim. For slow swimming, the otter moves its webbed feet in a dog-paddle. For greater speed, the otter holds its legs close to the body and flexes its whole body up and down. The flattened tail acts as a rudder.

LIFE IN THE FAST LANE

A leech has two suckers, which it uses to cling onto stones or water plants so it is not swept away by the current. Other adaptations to life in fast-flowing waters include the hooks of blackfly larvae and the flattened bodies of crayfish, flatworms, stonefly nymphs and mayfly nymphs. Some caddis fly larvae make cases around their bodies and stick themselves to stones or weight their cases down with pebbles.

Estuaries teem with worms, shellfish and crustaceans.

Kingfishers feed on fish, such as pike, carp and bream.

Otters and water voles make their nests in the middle river.

Trout like the oxygen here and can swim strongly against the current.

Caddis fly, mayfly and stonefly are common in upper rivers.

THE UPPER RIVER

Fast-flowing water contains plenty of oxygen but few plants for animals to eat.

THE MIDDLE RIVER

Here the river is wider, with a smooth layer of mud and silt covering the river bed. Plants take root along the river banks.

THE LOWER RIVER

When the river flows into the sea, it slows down and deposits mud and silt to form estuaries.

LAKE & POND DWELLERS

The still waters of lakes and ponds are comple and delicate ecosystems, where the balance of living things changes with the seasons, the climate and the water levels. They are easily upset by pollution, including increased nutrient levels from sewage and fertilizers, which encourage the growth of algae that block out the light and use up oxygen. In a clean pond or lake, there are three main zones: the pelagic zone of deep, open water in the middle, with algae, plankton and fish; the benthic or bottom zone, with algae, worms, larvae, and molluscs living in or on the mud; and the rich and varied littoral zone around the edge, with reeds and other rooted plants, together with a host of animals. Deeper lakes usually contain fewer animals than shallow ones but a greater variety of species. Lakes and ponds may freeze over in the winter but the wildlife survives in a layer of cold water trapped under the ice

DIVING BELL

The water spider is the only spider to spend its whole life underwater. It cannot take in oxygen from the water though, so it lives inside a bell-shaped web of silk, which it fills with air. It takes up to six trips to and from the surface to fill the silken bell with air. Once the diving bell is finished, the spider eats, mates and lays its eggs inside. It only leaves the bell to catch food.

FEATHERED FISHERMAN

The large and powerful great blue heron of North America often stands motionless at the edge of ponds and lakes watching for fish or frogs to come within reach. It may also stalk its prey; eventually spearing its catch with its long, sharp bill or using it like a pair of pincers to hold its prey. Most of these herons migrate south to warmer places in the winter.

WOOD DUCK

The beautiful iridescent colours of the male wood duck contrast sharply with

the camouflaged greys and browns of the female. Wood ducks live in lakes and ponds in wooded areas and nest in tree cavities or nest boxes. Soon after hatching, the young jump from the nest cavity down to the ground and follow their mother to the water.

POND MAKER

Beavers create ponds around their homes, called lodges, by building a dam of sticks and stones across a river. They know instinctively how to build their dams, which may be as tall as a person and up to 100 metres (328 ft) long. A beaver's pond is rather like a moat around a castle, helping to keep away predators, such as wolves and bears. A beaver can also use its pond to float logs and branches to the lodge and the dam.

UNIQUE SPECIES

Lakes are often home to unique species that develop in isolation, cut off from others of their own kind. Lake Victoria and Lake Tanganyika in East Africa are home to hundreds of different species of cichlid fish, like these guarding their nest from a terrapin. The different species can live together because they are adapted to eating different kinds of food.

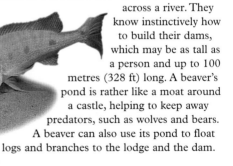

FILTERING FLAMINGOS

Flamingos wade into salty lakes to filter algae, small plants and animals from the water. They trap the food particles with comb-like plates on the bill. Flamingos live in large colonies, sometimes containing thousands of birds. They form a spectacular, but smelly, sea of pink on lakes such as Lake Nakuru in East Africa.

LOUDMOUTH GATORS

The largest reptiles in North America, alligators are also the loudest; the males bellowing particularly loudly in the breeding season. The sound carries for long distances, warning other males to keep away and telling females where they are. Alligators dig out large holes in the Everglades, which fill with water to provide a vital source for wildlife in the dry season. The alligators also feed on the wildlife, such as turtles and fish, sheltering in their gator holes.

RARE EGRET

The reddish egret hunts fish, frogs and crabs in the shallows of Florida Bay at low tide. It lurches, twists and turns through the shallows, dashing to the left and right in pursuit of its prey. Egrets, herons and ibises were hunted in the 1880s to supply feathers for the hat trade. In the 20th century, the birds have once again been threatened by destruction of their nesting and feeding areas and changes in water levels.

SPOON FEEDING

Nesting colonies of roseate spoonbills are a spectacular sight in the Everglades. They are named after their strange, spoon-shaped bill, which they use to feel for food in the muddy waters of the Everglades. They feed on small fish, shrimps and shellfish, snapping their bills shut when they touch their prey.

PRECIOUS PANTHER

Southern Florida is the last known refuge in the Eastern United States for the cougar – known in this area as the Florida panther. This beautiful predator is a powerful and expert hunter, jumping up to six metres (20 ft) in a single bound. The Florida panther needs a large territory in which to hunt mammals, such as deer. Although the Everglades is big, it may not be big enough to save the species. There are probably only about 30-50 animals left in the wild.

THE EVERGLADES

At the southern tip of Florida in the USA is a vast area of cypress swamp, mangroves and marsh called the Everglades. This famous wetland covers an area of some 5,490 sq km (2,120 sq miles) yet is only just above sea level. In the summer, higher water levels allow animals to move freely through the park. In the winter, they gather around the few remaining water holes. At least 300 types of bird, 25 mammals and 60 types of reptile can be found in the Everglades. The birds feed on the variety of insects and fish that live in this warm, humid environment. Several rare animals have taken refuge in the Everglades but, unfortunately, the park is threatened on all sides by agriculture, drainage schemes, buildings and people.

UNITED STATES
OF AMERICA

THE EVERGLADES

MUDDY MANGROVES

Where the Everglades meets the sea, the coasts are fringed with mangrove swamps. Mangroves are remarkable trees that are adapted to live in wet, salty places. Breathing pores in their roots take in oxygen from the air and help them to survive in waterlogged mud with little oxygen. Red mangroves like these protect the coast from storms and strong waves. They trap mud with their roots and new areas of land build up around them.

NESTING PREDATOR

The fish-eating osprey is a conspicuous resident of the Everglades. Its bulky stick nest is built on dead trees, floating buoys and telephone poles in the Florida Bay area or the mangrove wilderness. Ospreys are well adapted for catching fish, with sharp spines on their feet to grip hold of their slippery prey. They plunge feet-first into the water, grasping the fish in their strong talons.

MARSHES & SWAMPS

The difference between a marsh and a swamp is that a marsh is a wet grassland, while a swamp is a waterlogged forest with specially adapted trees, such as swamp cypress or mangroves. These extraordinary half-worlds – part land, part water, are usually associated with the edges of lakes, reservoirs, ponds, rivers or oceans where the waters become clogged with mud and a tangled, smelly mass of rotting plant and animal debris. Aquatic worms and crabs plough through the soft, slushy mud and water snails graze on the stems and leaves of water plants. The shallow, protected waters of swamps and marshes provide ideal nurseries for baby fish, tadpoles, insect larvae and the young of shellfish and shrimps. They are also an important feeding and breeding area for waterbirds, reptiles and mammals. Swampy areas act as natural reservoirs, collecting and holding water in the rainy season and releasing it during the dry season.

SWAMP STORKS

The magnificent saddle-bill stork is Africa's largest stork. It is named after the yellow 'saddle' on its upper bill. The long, pointed bill makes a formidable weapon for stabbing fish and other prey in the water. Its big feet disturb the fish as it wades through the water.

STRIPY SWIMMER

Several hundred tigers live in the Sundarbans, an enormous soggy swamp on the western edge of the Ganges, Brahmaputra and Megha river deltas in Bangladesh. The name Sundarbans means 'beautiful forest'. Dotted through the swamp are about 50 muddy islands covered with tropical forest, much of it submerged at high tide. The Sundarbans tigers hunt swamp deer, pigs, fish and crabs and share their swamp with a rich variety of animals, including crocodiles and monkeys.

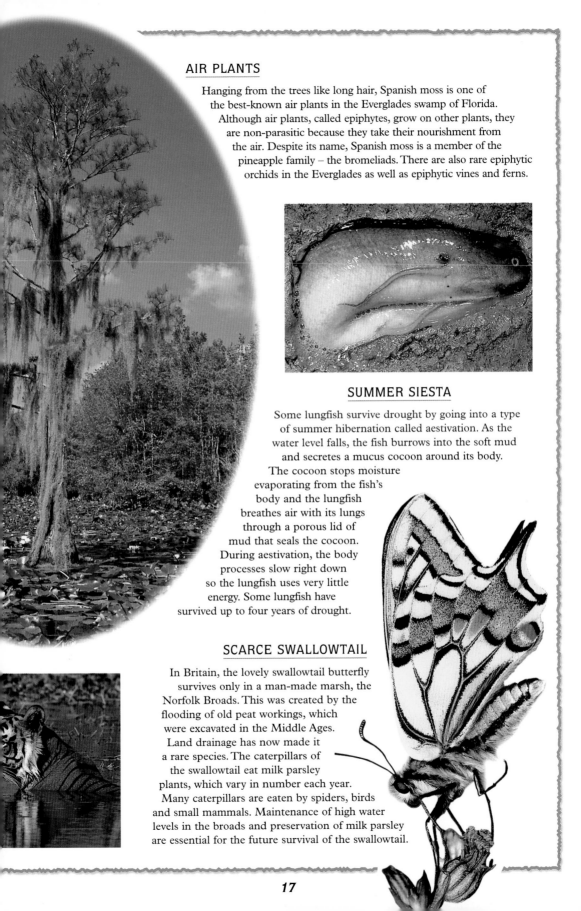

AIR PLANTS

Hanging from the trees like long hair, Spanish moss is one of
the best-known air plants in the Everglades swamp of Florida.
Although air plants, called epiphytes, grow on other plants, they
are non-parasitic because they take their nourishment from
the air. Despite its name, Spanish moss is a member of the
pineapple family – the bromeliads. There are also rare epiphytic
orchids in the Everglades as well as epiphytic vines and ferns.

SUMMER SIESTA

Some lungfish survive drought by going into a type
of summer hibernation called aestivation. As the
water level falls, the fish burrows into the soft mud
and secretes a mucus cocoon around its body.
The cocoon stops moisture
evaporating from the fish's
body and the lungfish
breathes air with its lungs
through a porous lid of
mud that seals the cocoon.
During aestivation, the body
processes slow right down
so the lungfish uses very little
energy. Some lungfish have
survived up to four years of drought.

SCARCE SWALLOWTAIL

In Britain, the lovely swallowtail butterfly
survives only in a man-made marsh, the
Norfolk Broads. This was created by the
flooding of old peat workings, which
were excavated in the Middle Ages.
Land drainage has now made it
a rare species. The caterpillars of
the swallowtail eat milk parsley
plants, which vary in number each year.
Many caterpillars are eaten by spiders, birds
and small mammals. Maintenance of high water
levels in the broads and preservation of milk parsley
are essential for the future survival of the swallowtail.

WATERY MOVEMENT

Many small water creatures just float or drift through the water, pushed along by the wind or water currents. Fish, frogs, water beetles and other larger animals use their muscles to propel themselves along. Water is much denser than air, so it supports an animal's weight but also holds it back as it tries to swim along. To make swimming easier, aquatic animals have a smooth, streamlined shape, a slippery surface and often webbed feet. Between the water and the air is a thin invisible 'skin', like a springy, bouncy platform. This forms on the surface of the water because water molecules are more attracted to each other than they are to the air above them and stick tightly together. To enable them to move on this surface skin, water walkers, such as pond-skaters, have special adaptations, such as waxy feet to repel the water and long legs to spread their weight.

WATER WALKER

Unlike small insects that really do walk on water, the African jacana or lily-trotter cheats by walking over floating lily pads instead. Its big feet, with their long, thin toes, work like the long legs of pond-skaters. They spread out the weight of the lily-trotter over a wide area and stop it sinking down into the water.

FROGGY PADDLE

At the first sign of danger, an adult frog will leap into the water. It can move faster through water than it can on land and there are plenty of places to hide among the water plants. The long, slim body of a frog and its rounded snout make it a streamlined shape for cutting through the water easily. Its webbed back feet are like the flippers we wear when snorkelling or diving. They push a lot of water out of the way at each stroke so the frog can swim fast.

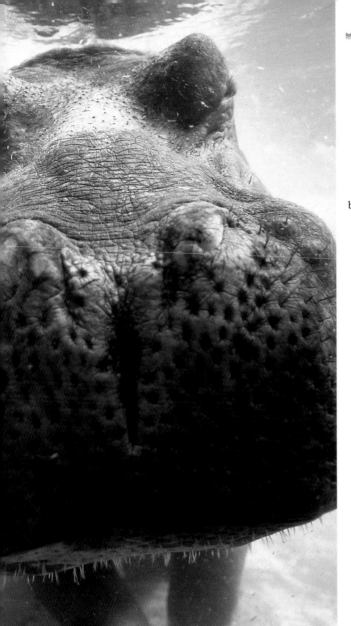

HAIRY OARS

Water boatmen are water bugs that live in ponds, canals and ditches. They have a streamlined, boat-shaped body and long, powerful back legs, which stick out of the sides of the body like oars. Hairs on the legs create a large surface area for brushing the water aside as the insect rows through the water.

UNDERWATER TANK

Looking rather like a giant underwater tank, the hippopotamus lumbers along the bottom of rivers, lakes and swamps. It is an excellent swimmer and diver and can stay underwater for up to five minutes. Hippos spend most of the daytime in the water because their skin loses water at a very high rate in air and they would rapidly dehydrate in the hot African sun. They are well adapted for an aquatic life. Water flows easily over their smooth skin, their webbed toes act like paddles, and they can close their nostrils and ears to keep the water out when they are underwater.

BLUE JEWEL

Kingfishers are shy birds, usually seen as a swift flash of bright blue speeding like an arrow along a river bank. To catch fish, the kingfisher dives headfirst into the water from a perch. Sometimes it will hover before diving. Once in the water (right), the kingfisher spears its prey in its dagger-like beak and holds it firmly until it gets back to the perch. There it beats its prey against a hard surface and swallows it headfirst. This makes sure the fish's fins and scales do not get caught in the bird's throat.

PREDATORS & PREY

ALGAE

↓

WATER FLEA

↓

STICKLEBACK

↓

PERCH

↓

HERON

Fish-eating waterbirds such as herons, kingfishers and storks are often the top predators at the end of wetland food chains. But these food chains often include more than one fish – big fish gobbling up smaller ones.

MASKED BANDIT

Mischievous raccoons use their long, mobile fingers for finding and catching aquatic prey, such as crayfish, fish, frogs and clams. They naturally tend to rub, feel and dunk their food in water, perhaps to investigate their prey or get rid of nasty skin secretions. Raccoons are more active in the evening than in the daytime and are good swimmers and climbers. The name raccoon comes from *arahkunem*, a Native American name for the animal. It means 'he scratches with his hands'.

Wetlands are full of tasty meals for predators to eat, especially water insects and fish. The biggest predators include alligators, crocodiles, anacondas, tigers and fish eagles. Some predators, such as snakes and otters, hunt in the water. Others, such as bats and fish eagles, swoop down to snatch a meal from the water's surface. Different techniques for catching prey include the surprise ambush of a crocodile, the high-speed chase of an otter, the stealthy stalk of a tiger or the tricky trap of a Venus flytrap plant. Mammals, such as otters and bats, together with reptiles, such as alligators and snakes, tend to hunt under cover of darkness. Birds, however, are daytime hunters. To catch and kill their prey, wetland predators rely on weapons such as sharp bills, teeth and talons as well as poisons and electric shocks.

PRISON BARS

The Venus flytrap is the most spectacular hunting plant, living only in one small patch of marshy country in Carolina, North America. Insects are attracted to the trap by its colour or the sweet nectar below the spikes. If they brush against special trigger hairs on the surface of the trap, the two halves snap shut in about a third of a second. The walls of the trap press tightly together and digestive juices dissolve the insect's body.

SHOOTING INSECTS

The remarkable archerfish spits drops of water up from the surface of the water to shoot down insects sitting on leaves above. If the insect falls into the water, the archerfish can snap it up. If the fish is only a few centimetres from the insect, it will jump out of the water and snatch the insect with its jaws rather than shoot it down.

FISHING EAGLE

The national bird of the USA, the bald eagle is a versatile predator of fish, birds and small mammals. It swoops down to the surface of the water to snatch fish in its strong, spiny talons. Groups of bald eagles also gather at salmon spawning grounds in Alaska, where the large number of dead and exhausted fish provide easy meals. This magnificent eagle is named after the white feathers on its head – an old meaning of the word bald.

FISHING SPIDER

Sitting on floating leaves or twigs with their front legs resting on the surface of the water, fishing spiders lie in wait for their prey. Hairs on their legs detect ripples in the water caused by fish swimming nearby. The spider can work out the position of a fish from the direction of the ripples and the distance between them. They kill their prey with a poisonous bite.

NORTH AMERICAN FOOD CHAIN

ALGAE

MOSQUITO LARVAE

BLUEGILL

FLORIDA SPOTTED GARFISH

ALLIGATOR

Wetland food chains rely on tiny floating plants in the water, which provide food for a variety of water insects. These, in turn, feed fish, which are preyed on by larger predators such as alligators and snakes.

DEFENCE

From armour and camouflage to poisons and chemical weapons, wetland animals use a variety of strategies to stay alive. For shoals of fish, flocks of waterbirds, herds of antelope or families of beavers there is safety in numbers. Many animals prefer to hide among the water plants, such as under lily pads or in-between the reeds along the water's edge. The sitatunga, an African antelope, submerges itself under the water if it senses danger, with only the tip of its nose protruding above the surface. Frightening enemies away is another survival tactic. Some animals display coloured markings, while snakes or crocodiles may hiss and puff up their bodies with air so they look bigger and more scary. Chemical weapons include poisons secreted by the skin of toads and salamanders, and acids sprayed by some caterpillars. Coming out at night helps some creatures, such as eels and moths, to avoid their predators.

FLASH COLOURS

Fire-bellied toads have undersides which are boldly marked with blotches of bright red, orange or yellow but the tops of their bodies are camouflaged with grey or green colours. To startle a predator, the toads suddenly expose their bright colours, giving themselves time to escape. The bright belly colours warn of poisonous skin secretions.

THE NUMBERS GAME

By keeping together, this shoal of minnows can help one another to spot danger. They also have less chance of being singled out for attack. Predators find shoals of fish confusing targets and most of the fish escape an attack.

CHAIN MAIL

The outside of a crocodile's or alligator's body is completely covered in tough scales and bony plates set into the thick, leathery skin. This coat of armour is rather like the coat of chain mail worn by medieval knights. Few predators will risk attacking a well-armoured adult crocodile, with its sharp teeth and powerful jaws. The crocodile's main enemy is people, who kill them for their skins, for food, or because they are dangerous.

CLEVER CAMOUFLAGE

Bitterns build their nests among reeds or sedges where they are well hidden and protected from enemies. These shy and secretive birds are very difficult to see in their marsh and swampland habitat. When threatened, a bittern often 'freezes' with its bill pointing straight up to the sky. The streaks on its breast feathers look just like the reeds and it may even sway back and forth like reeds in the wind.

HARMLESS HOGNOSE

The hognose snake of North America is harmless but it makes itself look frightening to scare away predators. First it widens its neck into a cobra-type hood. Then it hisses loudly and strikes towards the enemy. If all *that* does not work, the hognose snake smears itself all over with smelly scent and then rolls over and pretends to be dead. Predators prefer to eat live prey, so they leave the hognose snake alone.

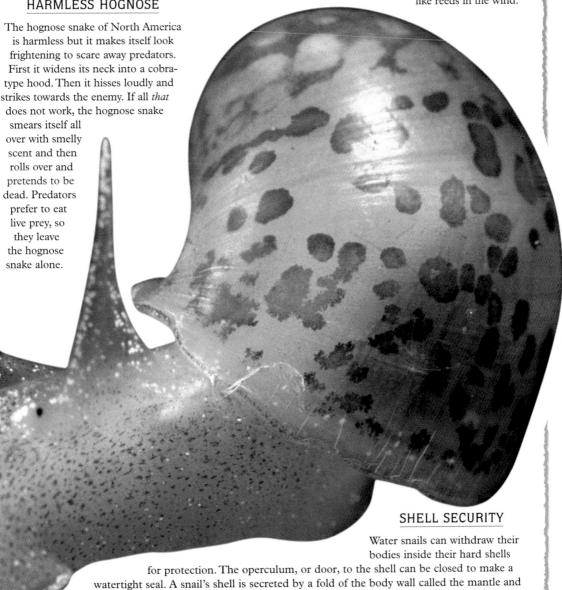

SHELL SECURITY

Water snails can withdraw their bodies inside their hard shells for protection. The operculum, or door, to the shell can be closed to make a watertight seal. A snail's shell is secreted by a fold of the body wall called the mantle and is made largely of calcium salts taken in from the water. The large shell of the great pond snail needs a lot of calcium carbonate so this species can only thrive in water containing plenty of lime.

NESTS, EGGS & YOUNG

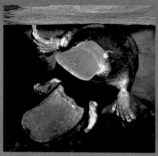

PECULIAR PLATYPUS

The duck-billed platypus is a very unusual mammal, unique to Australia, that lays eggs instead of giving birth to live young. The female lays two eggs at the end of a special breeding tunnel in a river bank, out of sight of predators. She curls herself around the eggs and incubates them for up to 14 days. The baby platypuses cut their way out of their eggs with an egg tooth. They feed on their mother's milk, which oozes out of her belly onto her fur.

The luxuriant plant growth of wetland habitats provides safe places for animals to lay eggs, build nests and give birth, while the shallow water areas contain plenty of food for the young to eat and calm water in which they can practise their swimming skills. Huge colonies of breeding birds, such as flamingos and herons, are found in wetlands. Some animals, such as frogs and dragonflies, spend part of their lives in the water and part on land. The eggs are laid in water and the young develop there, but the adults fly or move overland to new wetland areas. This helps to prevent inbreeding in small populations and prevents chance disasters wiping out whole populations.

A DOUBLE LIFE

Struggling to pull itself free of its larval skin, an adult dragonfly is about to begin its life as a hunter in the air. Eventually, it will mate and the female will lay her eggs in the water. The eggs hatch into larvae, which live underwater for between one and five years. The nymphs breathe through gills on the tips of their abdomens and feed mainly on aquatic invertebrates. They shed their skins several times as they slowly grow into adults. This gradual change to an adult form is called incomplete metamorphosis.

REED BASKET

The reed warbler's nest is a woven basket, fixed between dry reed stems above the wet reed bed. The nest is anchored with 'handles' and both male and female birds add grass, feathers and flowers on top to build up the nest. Reed warblers need considerable acrobatic skill because the reeds may constantly sway and wave about in the wind.

NESTING COUPLE

The male stickleback encourages a female to swim through his nest of waterweeds and lay her eggs. Then he will also swim through the nest and fertilize the eggs with his sperm. The male guards the nest closely, chasing away enemies and fanning a current of oxygen-rich water over the eggs with his front fins. Even after the young hatch, the male stickleback still keeps watch over his family, picking up in his mouth any that stray too far away.

FLAMINGO MILK

To make sure their chicks get enough food, flamingo parents produce a rich 'milk' in their crop – a kind of pouch in the wall of the gut. The milk is bright red because it contains red pigment from the food the birds eat. Their feathers also become pink or red for the same reason. When chicks are hungry, they make begging calls. Their beaks are straight at first and they have fluffy down feathers to keep them warm. Older chicks gather into a creche and are guarded by the adults in turn while other adults go off to feed.

LIVING TOGETHER

Animals living in a group help each other to look out for danger and take care of their young. A large source of food can cause animals, such as crocodiles, to congregate together. A drought can force groups to gather at water holes or any remaining source of water. Herons, egrets, storks and other wetland birds, gather together to nest in large colonies. Other animals, such as shoals of fish or herds of antelope or horses, live together all year round. Mammal societies often have a leader, such as a male zebra, leading a group of females and their young. Other family groups in wetlands include otter and beaver families. Sometimes, different kinds of animals live together and help each other to survive.

CROCODILE GATHERINGS

Crocodiles gather together in loose groups to bask in the sun, share food, court and nest. Groups, called pods, of young crocodiles hang out together and warn each other of danger. In times of drought, crocodiles of all ages gather together to share the water and avoid competing for scarce resources. Dominant crocodiles defend territories, which contain mates, basking sites, feeding places, nests and dens.

ZEBRA HERDS

Splashing across the Okavango swamplands in Africa, these Burchell's zebras protect themselves from predators by sticking together. Zebras live in family groups made up of females and their young, led by a strong male. Rival males will fight each other for control of a herd of females. The zebras communicate by means of sounds or body language, such as moving the position of the ears or the tail. Several families share a home range and may join in large herds, but family members can always recognize each other by voice, scent and the pattern of their stripes.

PIRANHA PACKS

Packs of red-bellied piranhas hunt through the tropical rivers of South America. In a matter of minutes they can strip the flesh off animals as large as goats that have accidentally fallen into the water. Meat-eating piranhas only turn to eating meat when plant food is hard to find. For most of the year they live on fruit and nuts that fall into the water.

PLANT LODGERS

The pitcher plants of marshes and bogs sometimes have animal lodgers living inside their pitchers. This one has a small tree frog sitting at the top, waiting to snap up insects before they fall down into the living trap. The twin-spurred pitcher has developed a small chamber in its stem that is regularly used by ants. As they steal a meal from the bottom of the pitcher, the ants accidentally help to chop up the pitcher's food.

HIPPO HERDS

During the day, hippos stay in the water in groups of about 10 or 15, made up of all-male bachelor groups or nursery groups. The nursery groups contain females and their young within the territories of a dominant male bull. Some bulls are solitary. In the evenings, the aquatic groups break up and the animals go ashore to feed. Other animals sometimes live with hippos, such as these oxpeckers that are feeding on tiny creatures on this hippo's skin.

PEOPLE & WETLANDS

People use wetlands in many ways – for fishing, farming, transport, tourism, recreation and sport.

The reeds from marshes are used for thatching or to make houses and boats, while peat bogs provide a source of fuel and garden soil. Transporting goods and people by water is still important in many parts of the world. Many people live near rivers and lakes and rely on them for their water supply. The energy from flowing water can also be used to make electricity. This is called hydroelectric power – 'hydro' means water. Unexpected floods can cause terrible problems for people living near rivers, such as the Mississippi in North America or the Huang Ho in China.

PEAT CUTTING

These men are cutting blocks of peat on the Outer Hebrides in Scotland to burn for fuel. They are using a special spade with a long handle and a thin blade, but peat is also dug with bulldozers and large mechanical diggers. Peat turves cut by hand are turned and stacked to allow them to dry before they are used. Peat is used to supply soil for gardens as well as for fuel. About 96% of Britain's peat bogs have been destroyed in the last 150 years. As well as affecting the wildlife, digging up peat releases carbon dioxide into the atmosphere and speeds up global warming.

BOAT TRAFFIC

Zooming through a North American swamp on an airboat is fun, but it disturbs the wildlife more than using boats without engines, such as canoes. The propellers from airboats can also injure wildlife, such as manatees in the Florida Everglades. Boat engines cause a lot of pollution and noise and the wash from boats can drown the eggs and chicks of birds nesting in the vegetation on the water's edge.

CROCODILE PEOPLE

The crocodile plays an important part in the myths and legends of the Iatmul people of the Sepik River in New Guinea. The saltwater crocodile was common in the mangrove swamps of the Sepik River basin and is believed by some peoples to be the creator of all living things. Its skull is kept in the men's spirit houses, such as this one, and the initiation ceremony for the young men involves cutting their

FLOODED FIELDS

In Asia, artificial wetlands are created when people flood fields to farm rice, which grows best when the plants are rooted in waterlogged mud. These flooded fields are called paddy fields and can also be used to farm frogs or fish, sometimes in pools next to the fields. This farmer is herding his geese across a rice paddy. People have grown rice in Thailand, China and India for at least 5,000 years.

CORMORANT FISHING

For centuries, cormorants have been used by people to help them catch fish. A ring is placed around the bird's neck to prevent it from swallowing the fish. When the cormorant comes to the surface, it is hauled to the boat on a special perch and the fish are taken out of its mouth. Later, the ring is removed so the cormorant can feed itself. Experienced birds can be trained to fish without the ring.

PROTECTING WETLANDS

The Camargue wetland in France is protected as a National Park but it is surrounded by industry and cities. Pollution seeps into the park wetlands, and large numbers of tourists may frighten and disturb the wildlife. Illegal hunting also goes on in the park. So even though a wetland may be protected, it still has to be managed very carefully, taking into account problems caused outside the protected area.

Wetlands are special places for wildlife, supporting perhaps a tenth of all the world's species. They are useful to people in all sorts of ways, as well as having a vital effect on the environment around them. Wetlands can help to control flooding by soaking up heavy rainfall and releasing it slowly. Mangrove swamps protect coasts from soil erosion and the effect of storms. In some places, wetlands also act as a form of natural pollution control, filtering the water that flows through them and removing impurities. On a global scale, peat bogs 'lock up' the carbon dioxide released by burning coal and oil and so help reduce global warming. About half the wetlands that once existed have been lost and those that remain urgently need our protection if they are to survive in the future. But leaving wetlands alone is not enough. Many would just silt up and disappear, so their water supply has to be carefully controlled.

MINING PROBLEMS

The Ranger uranium mine, on the edge of Kakadu National Park in Australia's Northern Territory, digs up uranium for the nuclear industry. Kakadu is a World Heritage Site of rivers, flood plains, creeks and billabongs spread over an area the size of Wales. It is home to many rare and unique species which are threatened by the presence of the mine.

CLEANING-UP WETLANDS

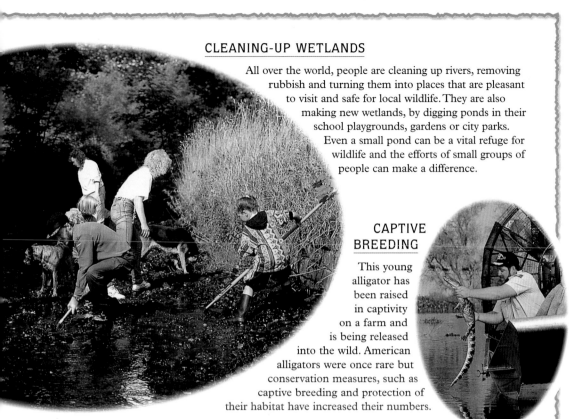

All over the world, people are cleaning up rivers, removing rubbish and turning them into places that are pleasant to visit and safe for local wildlife. They are also making new wetlands, by digging ponds in their school playgrounds, gardens or city parks. Even a small pond can be a vital refuge for wildlife and the efforts of small groups of people can make a difference.

CAPTIVE BREEDING

This young alligator has been raised in captivity on a farm and is being released into the wild. American alligators were once rare but conservation measures, such as captive breeding and protection of their habitat have increased their numbers.

RIVER MANAGEMENT

People build dams across rivers to control flooding, provide a water supply and generate electricity. But the dam changes the amount of water and sediment in the river and creates a huge artificial lake behind the dam. There may not be enough water downstream for people, farms, plants or animals. Changing the natural course of a river may actually cause flooding and other problems in the long term.

RARE SPECIES

The Spanish or Iberian lynx once occurred throughout Spain but now only a few hundred remain, mainly living in the Coto Doñana marshland reserve in southern Spain. This beautiful lynx has been reduced to near extinction by rapid economic development, with roads and agriculture destroying its natural habitat. It is now the world's most threatened cat species. Rare species like this can be protected by the preservation of their habitat, reducing any trade in their fur or other body parts, and captive breeding programmes.

FIND OUT MORE

Useful Addresses

To find out more about waterworlds, or the conservation of wetlands, here are some organizations that may be able to help.

YOUNG PEOPLE'S TRUST FOR THE ENVIRONMENT & NATURE CONSERVATION
95 Woodbridge Road, Guildford, Surrey, GU1 4PY

BRITISH HERPETOLOGICAL SOCIETY
c/o Zoological Society of London, Regents Park, London, NW1 4RY

FRESHWATER BIOLOGICAL ASSOCIATION
The Ferry House, Ambleside, Cumbria, LA22 OLP

FRIENDS OF THE EARTH
26-28 Underwood Street, London, N1 7JQ

WATCH TRUST FOR ENVIRONMENTAL EDUCATION
The Green, Whitham Park, Waterside South, Lincoln

WORLD WIDE FUND FOR NATURE
Panda House, Godalming, Surrey, GU7 1BR

THE BRITISH WATERFOWL ASSOCIATION
111 Lambeth Road, London SE1

Useful Websites

NATIONAL WETLANDS INVENTORY HOMEPAGE
www.nwi.fws.gov

THE WILDFOWL & WETLANDS TRUST
www.greenchannel.com/wwt/

WETLANDS FOR WILDLIFE
www.audubon.org/campaign/wetland/

NATIONAL WETLANDS PROGRAM
www.anca.gov.au/environm/wetlands/nwpindex.htm

ACKNOWLEDGEMENTS

We would like to thank: Helen Wire and Elizabeth Wiggans for their assistance. Artwork by Peter Bull Art Studio.
Copyright © 2000 ticktock Publishing Ltd.
First published in Great Britain by ticktock Publishing Ltd., The Offices in the Square, Hadlow, Tonbridge, Kent TN11 0DD, Great Britain.
All rights reserved.
No part of this publication may be reproduced, stored in a retrieval system, or transmitted in any form or by any means electronic, mechanical, photocopying, recording or otherwise, without prior written permission of the copyright owner.
A CIP catalogue record for this book is available from the British Library. ISBN 1 86007 147 3 (paperback). ISBN 1 86007 169 4 (hardback).

Picture research by Image Select. Printed in Hong Kong.

Picture Credits: t=top, b=bottom, c=centre, l=left, r=right, OFC=outside front cover, OBC=outside back cover, IFC=inside front cover

Oxford Scientific Films; 2ct, 2/3c, 3br, 3tr, 4tl, 4bl, 4/5t, 5cb, 6tl, 7br, 7c, 7cr, 8ct, 8/9c, 9t, 10bl, 10ct, 11cl, 12br, 13c, 16bl, 16/17t, 16/17b, 17cr, 17br, 18bl, 18tl, 19br, 19tr, 20/21t, 20/21b, 21cb, 22tl, 22c, 23b, 23tl, 23tr, 24cl, 24/25 (main pic), 25tr, 26/27b, 28ct, 30b, 30l, 30/31cb. Planet Earth Pictures; 24tl. Science Photo Library; 9b. Still Pictures; 6/7t, 8l, 12/13t. Tony Stone; OFC (main pic), OFC (inset pic) &12l, OBC & 28/29 (main pic), OBC & 31br, IFC & 20tl, 2l, 3cr, 5cr, 10/11c, 12l, 13tr, 13br, 14bl, 14tl, 14c, 14/15c, 15br, 15r, 18/19, 18/19cb, 21c, 22bl, 24/25t, 26l, 27tr, 27c, 28bl, 28/29b, 28/29t, 30/31t, 31cr, 31b.

Every effort has been made to trace the copyright holders and we apologize in advance for any unintentional omissions.
We would be pleased to insert the appropriate acknowledgement in any subsequent edition of this publication.

snapping-turtle
guide